LLAMAS:
Woolly, Winsome & Wonderful

by Susan L. Jones

©Copyright 1987, Susan L. Jones Photography
P.O. Box 1038
Dublin, Ohio 43017

Printed in the United States.

1 2 3 4   7 6 5 4

Library of Congress Cataloging-in-Publication Data

Jones, Susan L., 1943 —
    Llamas—woolly, winsome, and wonderful.

    Summary: Presents photographs of llamas with their
owners and discusses the gentle animal's history,
behavior, growth, and raising as a pet.
    1. Llamas as pets—Pictorial works. 2. Llamas—
Pictorial works. [1. Llamas as pets] I. Title.
SF459.L52J64   1987   636.2′96   87-29279
ISBN 0-942280-47-4

Book design: Barbara Fuller

This book is lovingly dedicated
to my husband Jack.

For many years I've been photographing llamas and translating their beauty to film. It has not been easy - good photography never is. I have succeeded in small part, however, if these photographs cause you to feel some of the beauty and excitement of llamas. And gentleness. For more than anything else, llamas have a gentle beauty that transcends our modern hectic world and carries us into that realm of peace and stability where we all wish to be.

Is that why they are magic?

Susan L. Jones
November 24, 1987

Sky Dancer, the llama pictured above, was raised on
a farm in Oregon. Some people are surprised to see Sky
Dancer on the farm because they think llamas live only
in zoos or in the mountains of South America. That was
true in the past, but it isn't true today. Many llamas are
raised on farms and ranches in the United States and
Canada.

Llamas make good pets because they are gentle animals. They have woolly bodies, pointed ears, and dark eyes with long lashes. They can wiggle their ears one at a time or both together.

Full-grown llamas are about the size of a large pony. Their coats can be brown, white, tan, black or gray. Most llamas have two or three colors. Some have bibs of color down their necks or circles around their eyes like a panda.

Spotted llamas are called "Appaloosas."

Baby llamas' colors and markings are often different from their parents' colors. It is always a surprise to see what colors a baby llama will be.

Females normally give birth to one baby a year, usually from a standing position. That is a long way for the baby to fall, but most babies walk and nurse soon after they are born.

When a baby is born, the other
llamas rush over to see the newborn.
They carefully inspect the baby and
sniff it with great curiosity.

New babies stay very close to their mothers.

Older babies often leave their mothers
to play. A favorite game is follow the
leader.

One baby will begin
running and jumping and the
rest will join in, copying the
movements of the one in
front.

When the babies get
hungry, they return to their
mothers.

Sometimes new babies are weak and need special attention. They may be fed milk from bottles and dressed in sweaters when it is cold.

Healthy babies don't need
protection from the cold. Their
wool coats keep them warm
enough.

Penelope was a baby llama who needed extra care and became a special pet for a farm girl named Carrie. Carrie nicknamed her llama "Penelope Pit Stop" because she never stopped racing unless she needed fuel, just like the race cars on television. When Penelope saw Carrie coming with her bottle, she ran so fast that it seemed she would crash into Carrie. At the last moment, Penelope would put on her brakes. Stretching her neck to reach the bottle, Penelope hummed while she ate, because she was happy. When Penelope was full, Carrie would cuddle her before she raced off again.

Llamas communicate by humming. To humans, all the hums sound much the same, but each baby knows its mother's hum. She might be saying, "Get back here where I can keep an eye on you!"

In warm weather, llamas enjoy sunbathing. They stretch out, lying flat and still, their necks and legs at odd angles like kids playing freeze tag. Llamas also enjoy dust baths. They roll in the dirt, jump up and shake their coats, making dust fly. Sometimes a baby jumps on top of its mother as she rolls. Baby llamas can be frisky and naughty.

A llama has no upper front teeth. It chews food with the teeth in the back of its mouth. Like a cow, the llama chews a cud. Cud is partially digested food that the animal stores in its stomach to chew at a later time. Animals that chew their cuds are called ruminants. Sheep and cows are ruminants too.

Llamas like to touch noses with each other and with their friends. Often they follow other animals or people just to see what's going on.

The llama is not a wild animal. It is called a domestic animal because it depends on people for its care and feeding.

At one time, llamas were found only in South America but today many llamas live on farms in the United States and Canada. There are llama farms in California, Colorado, Indiana, Alaska, New York, Oregon, Washington and many other states. Llamas are raised for their wool, to carry packs or to be pets. They are very gentle and make excellent pets.

There are about 12,000 llamas in North America. Raising llamas as a livestock animal is a new business for farmers and ranchers in our country.

This boy lives on a llama farm in Ohio. His name is
Elmer and like many other teenagers living on llama
farms he helps with the family herd.

Elmer's father and the veterinarian bring part of the herd to the corral so Elmer can catch a baby for a checkup. At 16, Elmer is almost totally in charge of the herd, and it's a big job! Elmer's father pays him for this work by giving him llamas to start a herd of his own.

Of all his farm chores, Elmer's favorite is training llamas to become pack animals. When they are two to three months old, babies begin wearing halters over their noses. At first they hate wearing the halters, but they soon get used to it. Then Elmer trains them to walk around on a lead rope. Two to three animals may be linked together so they will learn to walk together in a pack string. Llamas must know how to do this before they can become members of a packing outfit.

Pack llamas are used in national forests and parks to carry tents, sleeping bags and food for hikers and campers. Llamas can walk about ten miles a day over difficult trails, carrying a pack weighing up to eighty pounds. If they get tired or the pack is too heavy, llamas just lie down. And they won't get up again until they are rested or some of the weight is removed!

    Pack llamas wear a saddle and the packs are attached
to the saddle with hooks or rings. The weight must be
balanced on each side of the llama's body so each pack
is carefully weighed before it is attached to the saddle.

Even small children can handle a pack llama.

Llamas have soft pads instead of hard hooves like horses and mules so they don't damage wilderness trails as they walk and climb. This is important in camping areas where the trails can become damaged by overuse.

On the trail, llamas need very little food and water. Campers do not have to carry large amounts of food for their pack animals when they use llamas.

At night when it's time to pitch the tents, each llama is unloaded and tied to a stake with a long rope. This is called tethering and allows each animal to graze freely near camp.

Llamas are good "watch dogs" and will scream loudly to warn of danger if wild animals approach the camp.

When a llama is frightened it will run away or spit. Llamas in a zoo may spit at people who tease or frighten them. But llamas that are well cared for and not teased do not spit, bite or kick at people. They have loveable personalities and they won't spit unless you spit first!

However, llamas do spit at each other. They're saying, "Keep your nose out of my pile of hay," or "Stop hogging all the fresh water!"

When llamas lower their ears, watch out - usually that means they are unhappy and ready to spit.

Llamas may be sheared every two years.
Llama wool is thick and colorful.
Spinners turn it into soft, strong yarn
for weaving or knitting blankets, hats,
sweaters and coats.

Sheared llamas are not very pretty, and a new coat takes a long time to grow. Many owners don't shear their llamas but gather wool by brushing. The brushed wool is collected and stored in a sack or bag.

After brushing, many owners groom their animals
with an electric blower, which removes more dust and
dirt and leaves the wool fluffy and clean.

Llama owners do lots of fun things with their animals. Llamas are easily trained and seem to enjoy going to different places. They can climb in a van or pickup truck and ride with people.

Llamas also compete in pack races. Each llama carries a pack weighing thirty pounds and is led by a runner across streams, up and down hills and over rocky mountain trails. The fastest team wins the race.

This is a "flap-jack" race. Each team races to a spot
where the trainer must start a fire and cook a pancake.
The llama must stand quietly while its trainer cooks.
The first person to build a fire, mix up some batter and
cook a pancake, wins.

This llama is learning to pull a cart.
This is called "driving."

Once a llama is trained to drive, he can join a driving team and help to pull a large wagon.

Llamas go to school for "show and tell."

Run in cart races....

And dress up for Halloween and Christmas.

In 4-H clubs, children learn about llamas and practice showing their animals. This helps the children and their pets win ribbons at llama shows.

Llamas have many uses, but the best
use of all is to love them.

A SHORT HISTORY OF LLAMAS

The ancestors of the llama lived in North America about 40 million years ago. These ancestors were members of the camel family, collectively known as camelids, a family that was confined to North America until just before the last Ice Age.

About one million years ago, the camelids began to migrate from North America. Some crossed the Bering land bridge into Eurasia where they evolved into dromedary (one-hump) and Bactrian (two-hump) camels. Others wandered into South America and evolved into vicunas and guanacos. Alpacas and llamas were domesticated from these two camelids.

About six million llamas live in South America today. The llamas' original range in the Andes Mountains of Bolivia and Peru is known as the **altiplano**—or high plateau. There, the high altitude caused an amazing evolutionary adaptation in llamas: they use oxygen more efficiently than other animals and their red blood cells have a longer life span, 235 days as compared to 100 for a human.

In the Central Andes Mountains, alpacas and llamas are the Indian's all-purpose animals. Males are used for packing heavy loads. Females are kept for breeding. The wool is shorn and woven into clothing. The droppings are used as fuel, and the milk is made into a rich yogurt. Older animals are eaten for food and their hides are made into leather products.

In North America the last of the camelids died out toward the close of the Pleistocene, about 10,000 years ago. Llamas did not return until the early part of the nineteenth century when two men, both animal collectors, began to import them from South America and from European zoos to raise on their game farms. These men, Roland Lindemann and Randolph Hearst, were primarily responsible for most of the llama importation into the United States until the late 1930's. Their herds are the ancestors of most llamas in North America today. It is estimated that the llama population in North America ranges from 12,000 to 15,000 animals.

Llamas are hardy and will thrive if they receive little more than fresh water and a good quality hay. A full-grown llama needs about four and a half pounds of hay each day. Llamas also adapt well to small amounts of space. Four or five adults can be kept on an acre of pasture. Breeders follow different inoculation routines, depending on what livestock health problems are prevalent in their part of the country.

At the present time, there is only one real drawback to owning llamas—there are just not enough to go around.

Sources of more information about llamas:

The International Llama Association, P.O. Box 37505, Denver, CO 80237. There are eleven chapters of the ILA. Contact the central office for geographic locations.

The Llama Association of North America, P.O. Box 1174, Sacramento, CA 95806.

Llamas Magazine, P.O. Box 100, Herald, CA 95638.

Rocky Mountain Llama Association, 15251-6100 Road, Montrose, CO 81401.